MW00559142

BOOK 7

SIGHT READING & RHYTHM EVERY DAY®

Helen Marlais with Kevin Olson

THE
F·J·H
MUSIC
COMPANY
INC.
Frank J. Hackinson

Production: Frank J. Hackinson
Production Coordinators: Peggy Gallagher and Philip Groeber
Editor: Edwin McLean
Contributing Editor: Jordan Waller
Cover: Terpstra Design, San Francisco
Text Design and Layout: Terpstra Design and Maritza Cosano Gomez
Engraving: Tempo Music Press, Inc.
Printer: Tempo Music Press, Inc.

ISBN-13: 978-1-61928-096-0

ABOUT THE AUTHORS

Dr. Marlais is one of the most prolific authors in the field of educational piano music and an exclusive writer for The FJH Music Company Inc. The critically acclaimed and award-winning piano series: *Succeeding at the Piano® –A Method for Everyone, Succeeding with the Masters®, The Festival Collection®, In Recital®, Sight Reading and Rhythm Every Day®, Write, Play, and Hear Your Theory Every Day®*, and *The FJH Contemporary Keyboard Editions*, among others, included in *The FJH Pianist's Curriculum®* by Helen Marlais, are designed to guide students from the beginner through advanced levels. Dr. Marlais gives pedagogical workshops worldwide, and the method *Succeeding at the Piano®* is published in South Korea and Taiwan. She presents showcases for The FJH Music Company at national conventions and internationally.

Dr. Marlais has performed and presented throughout the U.S. and in Canada, Jamaica, Italy, England, France, Hungary, Turkey, Germany, Lithuania, Estonia, Australia, New Zealand, China, South Korea, Taiwan, Jamaica, and Russia. She has recorded on Gasparo, Centaur and Audite record labels with her husband, concert clarinetist Arthur Campbell. Their recording, *Music for Clarinet and Piano,* was nominated for the 2013 *International Classical Music Awards,* one of the most prestigious distinctions available to classical musicians today. She has also recorded numerous educational piano CD's for Stargrass Records®. She has performed with members of the Chicago, Pittsburgh, Minnesota, Grand Rapids, Des Moines, Cedar Rapids, and Beijing National Symphony Orchestras, and has premiered many new works by contemporary composers from the United States, Canada, and Europe.

Dr. Marlais received her DM in piano performance and pedagogy from Northwestern University, her MFA in piano performance from Carnegie Mellon University, and was awarded the Outstanding Alumna in the Arts from the University of Toledo, where she received her bachelor of music degree in piano performance. As well as being the Director of Keyboard Publications for The FJH Music Company, Dr. Marlais is also an Associate Professor of Music at Grand Valley State University in Grand Rapids, Michigan. Visit: www.helenmarlais.com

Kevin Olson is an active pianist, composer, and member of the piano faculty at Utah State University, where he teaches piano literature, pedagogy, and accompanying courses. In addition to his collegiate teaching responsibilities, Kevin directs the Utah State Youth Conservatory, which provides weekly group and private piano instruction to more than 200 pre-college community students. The National Association of Schools of Music has recently recognized the Conservatory as a model for pre-college piano instruction programs. Before teaching at Utah State, he was on the faculty at Elmhurst College near Chicago and Humboldt State University in northern California.

A native of Utah, Kevin began composing at age five. When he was twelve, his composition, *An American Trainride,* received the Overall First Prize at the 1983 National PTA Convention at Albuquerque, New Mexico. Since then he has been a Composer in Residence at the National Conference on Keyboard Pedagogy, and has written music commissioned and performed by groups such as the American Piano Quartet, Chicago a cappella, the Rich Matteson Jazz Festival, MTNA (Music Teachers National Association), and several piano teacher associations around the country.

Kevin maintains a large piano studio, teaching students of a variety of ages and abilities. Many of the needs of his own piano students have inspired more than 100 books and solos published by The FJH Music Company Inc., which he joined as a writer in 1994.

HOW THE SERIES IS ORGANIZED

All rhythmic activities

All sight-reading activities

All Rhythm Flash!, Pattern Flash!, Interval Flash!, & Chord Flash! activities

Place a ✔ when you have been successful!

Each unit of the series is divided into five separate days of enjoyable rhythmic and sight-reading activities. Students complete these short daily activities "Every Day" at home, by themselves. Every day the words, "Did It!" are found in boxes for the student to check once they have completed both the rhythm and sight-reading activities.

The new concepts are identified in the upper right-hand corner of each unit. Once introduced, these concepts are continually reinforced through subsequent units.

On the lesson day, there are short rhythmic and sight-reading activities that will take only minutes for the teacher and student to do together. An enjoyable sight-reading duet wraps up each unit.

BOOK 7

Rhythm:

Rhythmic activities in book 7 include the following:

- Internalize rhythms in many ways by clapping, tapping, and stomping on the floor, and snapping.
- Metronome markings are often given so that students can practice at different tempos and be consistently steady.
- Review of sixteenth-note rhythms and their variants.
- Review of triplet rhythms.
- Review of $\frac{2}{4}$, $\frac{3}{4}$, $\frac{4}{4}$, and $\frac{6}{4}$ time signatures.
- New to this level is the understanding of sixteenth-note rhythms and their variants in $\frac{3}{8}$ and $\frac{6}{8}$ time signatures.
- Lyrics spoken in rhythm.
- Adding bar lines and writing missing rhythms into excerpts and then counting the examples out loud.
- Tapping different rhythms in each hand.
- Clapping rhythmic examples by memory—an excellent ear training and memory exercise.
- "Rhythm Flashes"—short rhythmic patterns that students look at briefly and then tap by memory. This skill helps them to think and prepare quickly.

Fingering:

A modest amount of fingering is provided so that students learn to think for themselves. Students sometimes are asked to decide their own fingering and write it directly in the score before starting to play.

Tips for Sight Reading:
- Decide the time and key signature.
- Look for patterns in the music (intervals, phrases, rhythms).
- Sing or hum the piece in your mind.
- Plan the fingering.
- Make sure you count the rhythm at a steady tempo before starting.
- Plan the sound before you play.

Tips when playing:
- Sight read at a tempo that you can keep steady, without stopping.
- Keep your eyes on the music, not on your hands.
- Play musically and don't worry about mistakes. Concentrate on keeping the tempo.

Tips when playing: continued
- Make use of the metronome.

Reading:

Pieces are sight read using augmented and diminished chords, and pieces using dominant seventh chords. Review of major and minor scales, major and minor first and second inversion triads, and cadences. Syncopated pedaling is continued. Students review relative major and minor keys—C/Am, D/Bm, E/C♯m, F/Dm, G/Em, B♭/Gm, E♭/Cm, A♭/Fm, A/F♯m. Syncopation, improvisation, tempo markings, waltz bass, Alberti bass, and broken-chord bass are reviewed.

Three-part chorales are found throughout this level as well as a review of intervals (2nds through octaves). Students are asked to focus on balancing melodies over simple accompaniments and play harmonizations where the left hand plays harmony and the right hand plays a melody. Duet playing as a Lesson Day activity continues to further reinforce the importance of continuity when sight reading.

Sight-Reading activities include the following:

- Students are asked to transpose short pieces to other keys, and continue to review ledger line reading as well as play pieces with changing clefs and ledger lines.
- Students focus on accuracy as well as quick thinking in "Interval Flashes!" "Chord Flashes!", and "Pattern Flashes!" These short patterns that are played, or looked at briefly and then played by memory further help students to look ahead and think and prepare quickly.
- Learning to "plan" for note and rhythmic accuracy, correct articulations, and a good sound.
- "Hearing" what the music is supposed to sound like before starting to play.
- Helpful suggestions that guide students to think before playing and not to stop once they have started.
- Singing or humming the melody of some of the excerpts, which encourages listening while maintaining a constant pulse and the forward motion of the musical lines.
- Planning intervals, patterns, and crossovers before playing and frequent use of the metronome.

FJH224

TABLE OF CONTENTS

Sight Reading and Rhythm Review - Let's Get Started!

It's True or False Time!

How well do you know the basics of excellent sight reading?

Write True or False next to each statement.

1. It's important to listen to yourself play. _____

2. It's important to look at the time and key signatures before you start a piece. _____

3. It's fine to stop and start throughout a piece, just to get everything right. _____

4. It's important to look for patterns in the music, such as intervals, chords, melodic patterns, phrases, and rhythm. _____

5. It's good to look at your music and down at your hands often, so that you are sure that you have all of the moves and jumps correct. _____

6. As you play, it's important to look ahead and not stop for any mistakes. _____

7. It's a good idea to think of other things you need to do during the day while sight reading. _____

8. No matter what, keep the tempo steady and don't stop while you play. _____

9. It's important to look over the score, planning what is the same and what is different, the fingering, and the sound of the piece. _____

10. It's good to count your mistakes so that you will do better in the future. _____

11. It's a good idea to use the metonome when you practice sight reading to make a habit of keeping the beat steady. _____

12. Being a good sight reader is a gift. It's not a skill that you can learn. _____

Answers: 1. True 2. True 3. False 4. True 5. False 6. True 7. False 8. True 9. True 10. False 11. True 12. False

Sight Reading and Rhythm Review - Let's Get Started!

What is the key? _____ Prepare the Alberti bass and the move before playing.

Transpose to: C minor____

Find and play the major and augmented triads before playing hands together.
What is the last note? _____

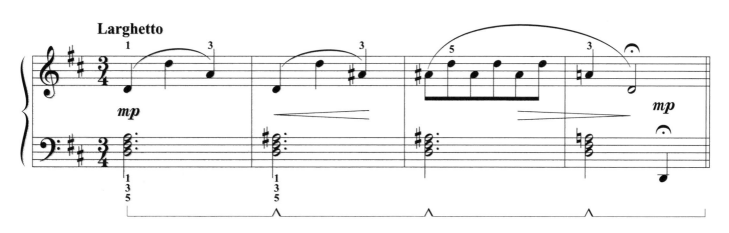

Transpose to: E Major____   F Major____

Find and play the minor and diminished triads before playing hands together.

Transpose to: E minor____   F minor_____   G minor_____

Unit 1

New Concept: sixteenth notes in 3/8 and 6/8 time.
Review of relative keys of C major and A minor

 Rhythm—Clap and count aloud with energy! Then choose a major scale and play this example on the piano. ♪ = 108

Place a ✔ when you have been successful!

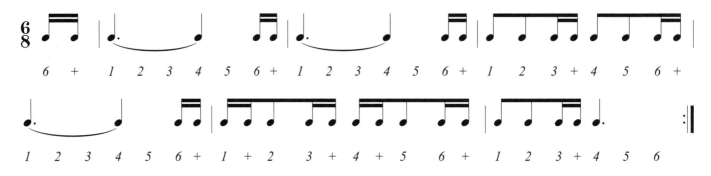

 Rhythm Flash! Clap and count the first example, then close the book. Clap it again from memory. Then try the second example.

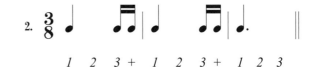

 Sight reading—Silently play this piece hands separately, then hands together. Always look ahead and play with a steady rhythm.

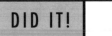

FJH224

Rhythm—Clap and count the following rhythm out loud. Then say the words while pointing to each note.

DID IT!

Interval Flash!—Review the following examples. Then play while saying the intervals.

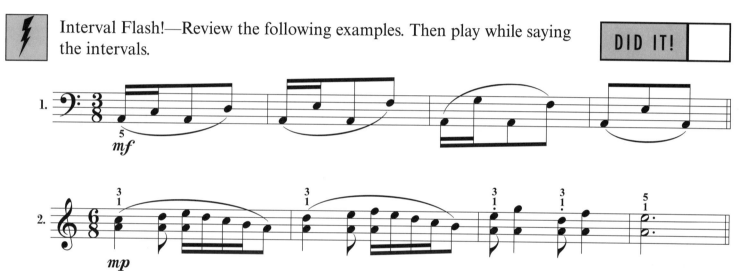

DID IT!

Sight reading—Silently plan the fingering and the chords in the left hand.

DID IT!

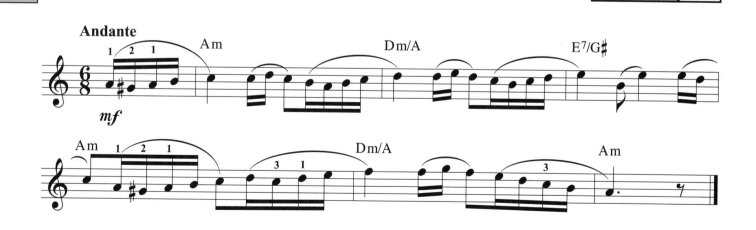

Rhythm—Clap and count the following example with energy in your voice! ♪ = 108.

 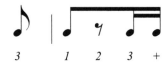  

 Sight reading—Silently review the intervals in the right hand and plan your fingering. Then play it hands together.

Key of _____

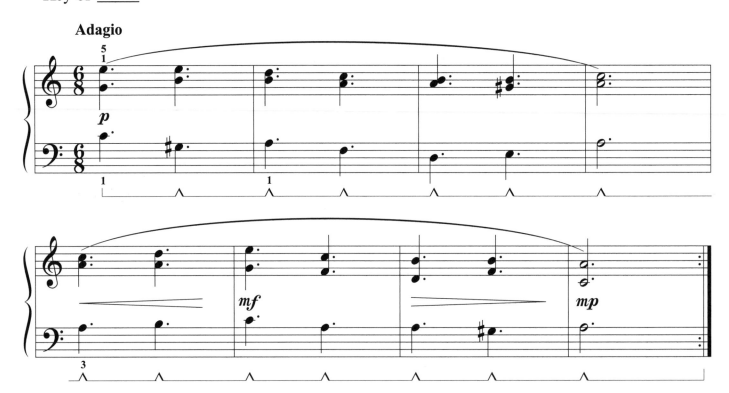

FJH224

Rhythm—Add bar lines to the following example. Then clap and count aloud with energy.

DID IT!

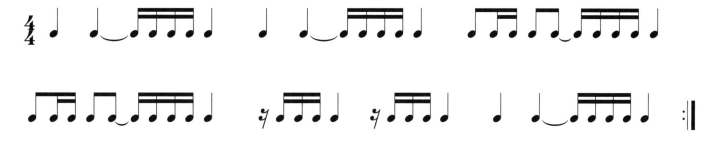

 Sight reading—Plan a tempo that you can keep steady. Then play it with confidence!

DID IT!

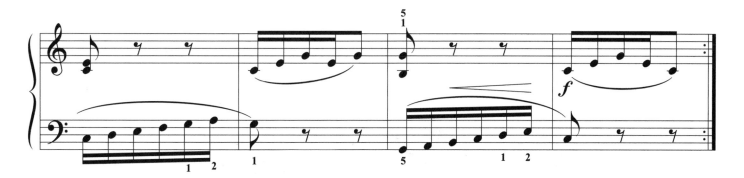

Rhythm—Slap the rhythm of your right hand and stomp the rhythm of your left hand. Keep it slow and steady. ♪ = 160

DID IT!

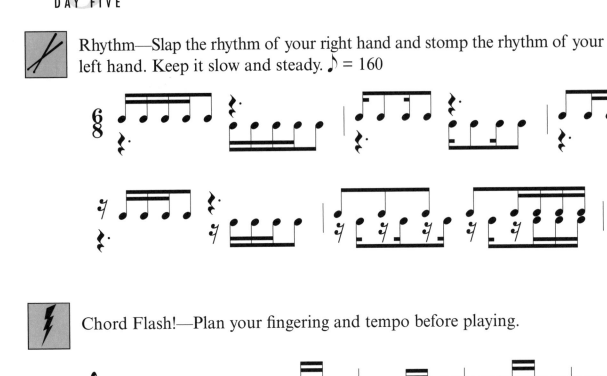

Chord Flash!—Plan your fingering and tempo before playing.

DID IT!

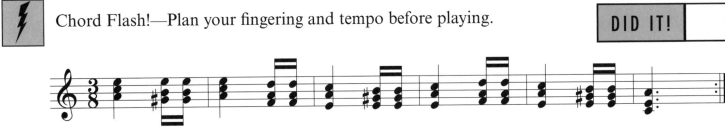

Sight reading—Play the right hand as blocked chords. Then play as written, looking ahead.

DID IT!

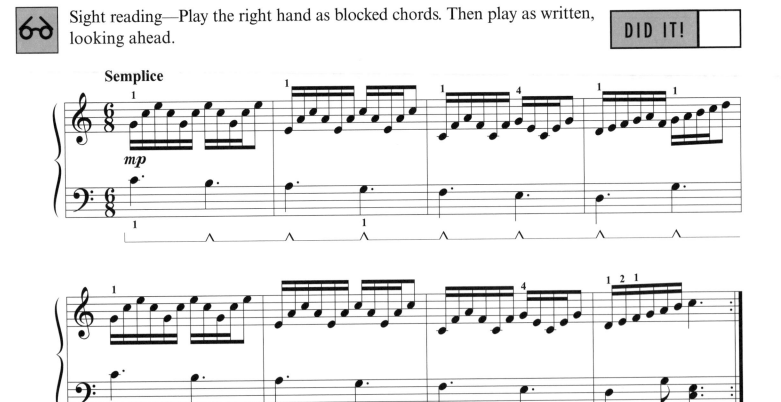

FJH224

Ensemble Piece

DID IT!

Look for patterns in the music before you begin.

Wintry Sunset

Teacher accompaniment (student plays as written)

? After playing, ask yourself, "Did the rhythm feel easy?"
If so, great! If not, play it until it's easy.

Unit 2

Review of relative keys of D major and B minor

Rhythm—Count and clap with complete steadiness. When you see a note with an "X," snap your fingers.

DID IT!

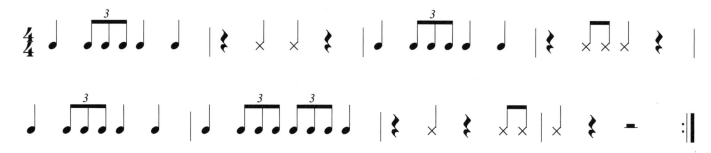

Interval Flash!—Look at the following example for 10 seconds or less. Then play it! Close the book and play it again from memory.

DID IT!

Sight reading—Silently review the right-hand intervals. Play without looking at your hands.

DID IT!

Key of _____

FJH2241

Rhythm—Tap the following rhythm with the metronome set at ♩ = 96.

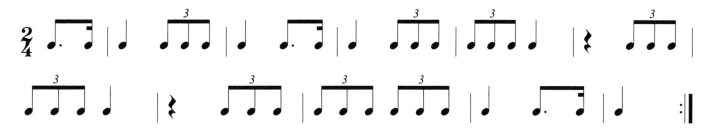

Pattern Flash!—Look at the pattern for 10 seconds. Then play it and continue the sequence for an octave.

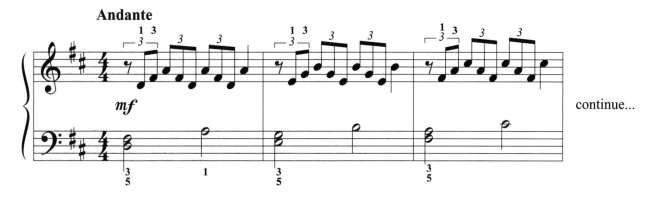

continue...

Sight reading—Tap the right-hand rhythm and plan the left-hand chords. Then play it with confidence!

Rhythm—Tap and count the following rhythm with both hands, evenly and accurately. ♩=84.

DID IT!

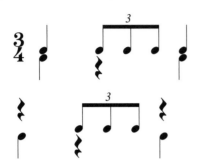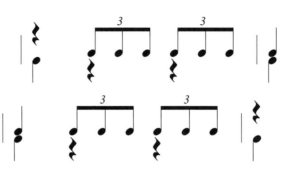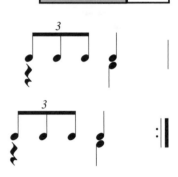

Chord Flash!—Quickly review the following chords. Then play with a steady rhythm. Can you play them with your eyes closed?

DID IT!

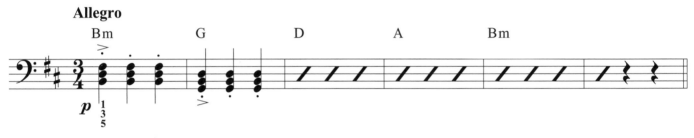

Before beginning, choose a tempo that you know you can keep steady.

DID IT!

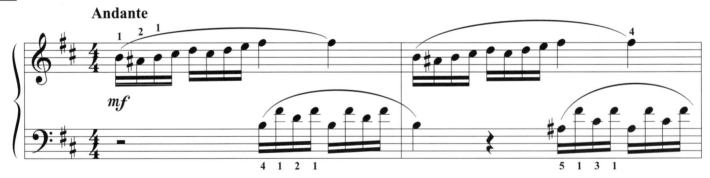

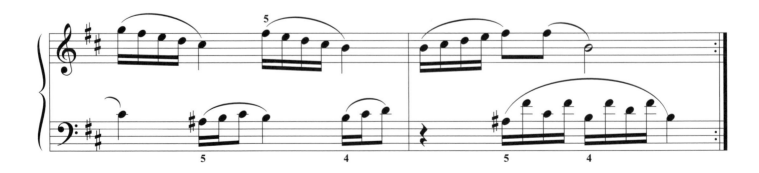

FJH224

Rhythm—Add bar lines to the following example. Then tap the underside of the piano while holding down the pedal.

♩ = _____ (try ♩ = 72 or slower)
your choice

 Silently play on the top of the keys. Once you begin, don't stop until the very end.

Rhythm—Fill in your own rhythm for the blank measures. Then tap and count aloud with energy in your voice! Lastly, play this rhythm using the notes of the B♭ major scale!

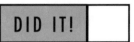

 Interval Flash!—Plan the fingering. Block the triplet first. Then play as written. Do the same for the second example.

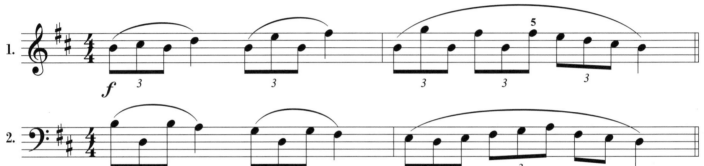

 Sight reading—Play with the triplets blocked, planning the accidentals as you go. Then play as written with complete steadiness.

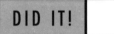

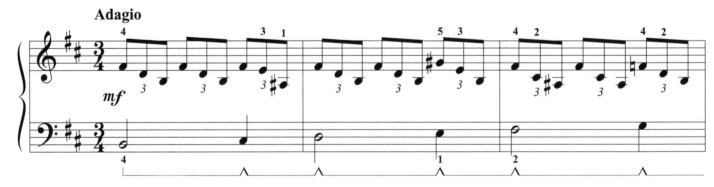

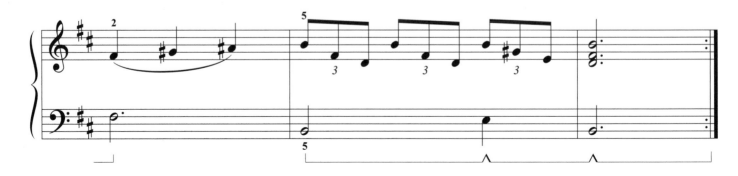

FJH224

Ensemble Piece

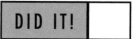
Look at the rhythm in m. 5 as compared to the rhythm at the beginning. At ♩ = ca. 60, tap the rhythm, hands together. Then block the right-hand chords. Can you sing the L.H. melody while you play?

Twinkle, Twinkle, Pachelbel

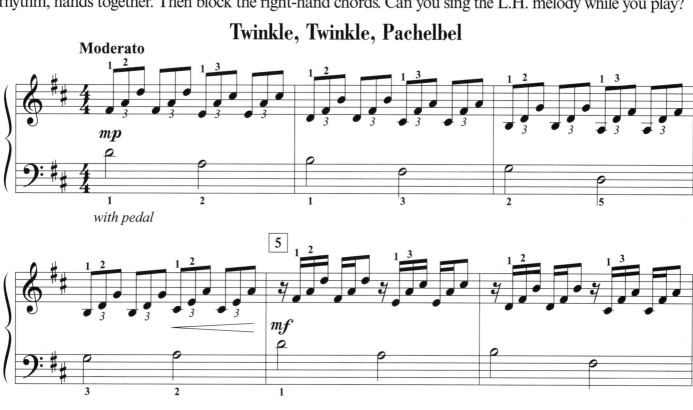

Teacher accompaniment (student plays as written)

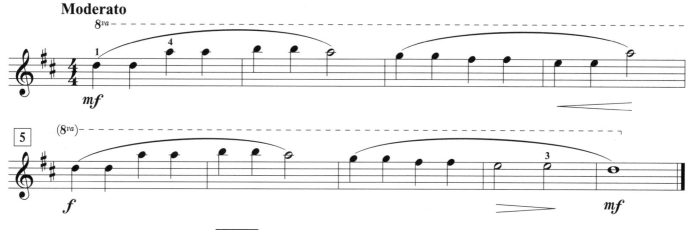

? After playing, ask yourself, "Did I listen to my teacher's part to lock in the rhythm?"

Unit 3

Rhythm—Tap and count the following example with complete evenness and accuracy. ♪ = 104

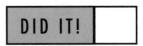

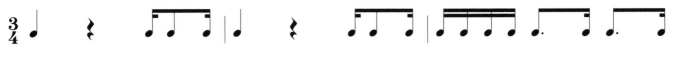

Rhythm Flash!—Look at the following example for 10 seconds or less. Then close the book and tap the rhythm from memory.

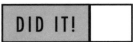

Sight reading—Tap the rhythm, hands together. Plan the key and a steady tempo before playing. "Hear" the rhythm of the left hand before playing.

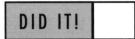

Key of _____

FJH224

Rhythm—Clap and count with energy! ♪ =108. Then play the rhythm using the notes of an E major scale.

DID IT!

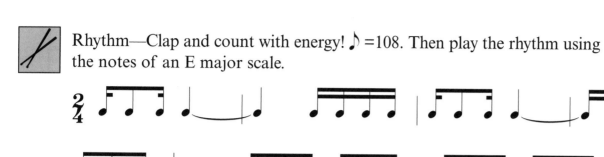

Pattern Flash!—Tap the rhythm. Then plan the key and play! Play the pattern at least six times.

DID IT!

Sight reading—Think through the piece while counting before playing. Can you sing the right-hand melody?

DID IT!

Key of _____

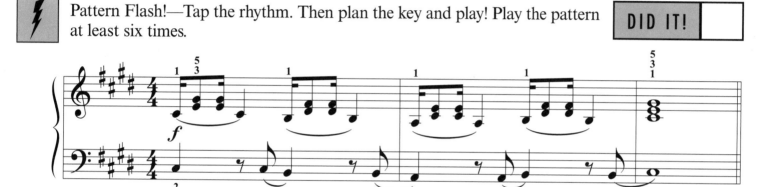

Rhythm—Tap this rhythm on your thighs. Then choose any two notes in the C# minor scale and play it without stopping.

DID IT!

Chord Flash!—Block the chords first. Plan your fingering. First play each example f, then pp.

DID IT!

Sight reading—Prepare the right-hand chords. Then tap the rhythm, hands together. Play at a tempo you can keep steady, counting aloud as you play.

DID IT!

FJH2241

Rhythm—Tap and count the rhythm aloud. Then say the following lyrics while pointing to each note. **DID IT!**

Four score and sev-en years a-go our fa-thers brought forth on this con-ti-nent a

new na-tion, con-ceived in li-ber-ty, and ded-i-cat-ed to the prop-o-si-tion that

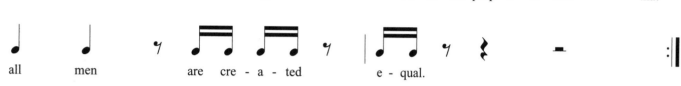

all men are cre-a-ted e-qual.

 Pattern Flash!—Take 20 seconds or less to tap the rhythm. Then play with a steady tempo. Name the chords as you play (C#m, A, B, C#m). **DID IT!**

 Sight reading—Tap the rhythm and then play it silently on the top of the keys while counting. Lastly, play it! **DID IT!**

Rhythm—Fill in the blank measures with your own combination of ♪ and ♪
notes and rests. Then stomp or tap the rhythm.

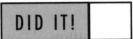

 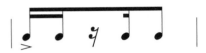

Rhythm Flash!—Tap and count. Can you tap it a 2nd time from memory?

Sight reading—Tap the following rhythm hands together. Plan the key
and the tempo.

FJH224

Ensemble Piece

DID IT!

Before playing as written, tap and count the rhythm, hands together. Observe the key signature and the intervals. Which hand should play louder?

Key of _____

Heroic Voyage

Teacher accompaniment (student plays as written)

After playing, ask yourself, "Did the duet sound heroic?"

Unit 4

Review of relative keys of F major and
D minor

 Rhythm—Tap and count the following example with energy in your voice! ♪ = 120, then ♩ = 104.

DID IT!

Rhythm Flash!—Look at the following rhythm for 10 seconds. Then close the book and tap it from memory.

DID IT!

 Sight reading—How are the patterns in each measure similar? Think the rhythm through before playing. Can you sing the right-hand scales?

DID IT!

Key of _____

Rhythm—Write in the rest of the counting. Clap with the metronome at ♩ = 76. Focus on keeping the ♩ steady.

DID IT!

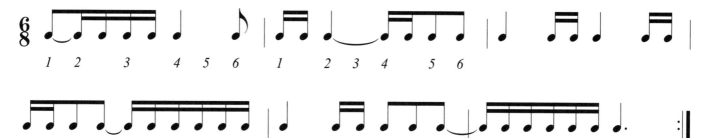

 Pattern Flash!—Play steadily. Then close your eyes and play it again from memory. How did you do? Good_____ Not so good_____ (check one)

DID IT!

 Sight reading—Play the left hand first. Then, play hands together at a tempo you can be successful with.

DID IT!

Key of _____

Tempo di Tango

Rhythm—Add notes and rests to the incomplete measures. Improvise a melody in the key of F major using the following rhythm. Count while you play!

Interval Flash!—Say the intervals while you play the first example. Then do the same with the second example.

Sight reading—Play only the downbeats. Can you name the chords in the right hand? Once you begin this piece, don't stop until the very end.

FJH224

Rhythm—Tap the following rhythm evenly and accurately.　　DID IT! ☐

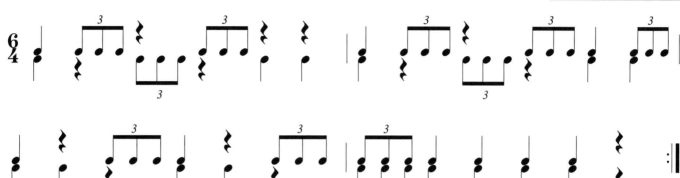

 Pattern Flash!—Plan the fingering. What is the key? After you play it once, close the book and try to play it again from memory.　　DID IT! ☐

 Sight reading—First, silently plan the left-hand chords. Then play hands together at a tempo you can keep steady.　　DID IT! ☐

Rhythm—Tap this rhythm on the fallboard of the piano evenly! When you see an "X," snap your fingers.

DID IT!

 Sight reading—Block the right hand, planning the intervals and accidentals before you begin. Then block hands together, and lastly play as written.

DID IT!

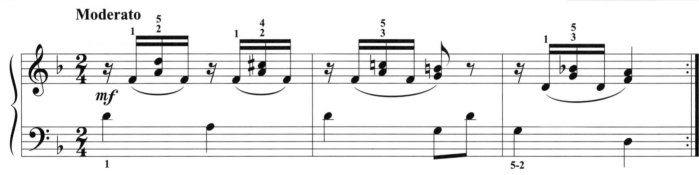

 Sight reading—Plan the fingering, the chords, and the tempo before starting. Block hands together to understand the descending pattern.

DID IT!

FJH2241

Ensemble Piece

DID IT!

Before playing, plan the key and the time signature. Silently play on the top of the keys while counting aloud. Your teacher will give you two minutes to prepare.

Key of _____

Shepherd's Flute

Teacher accompaniment (student plays as written)

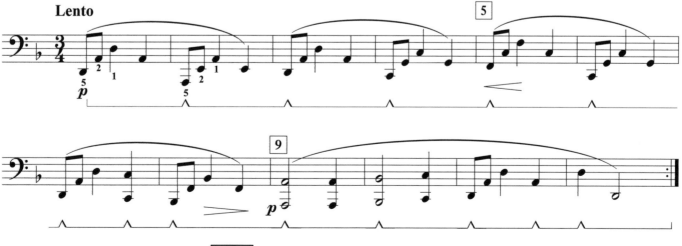

? After playing, ask yourself, "Was the piece calm and gentle?"

Unit 5

DAY ONE

Review of relative keys of G major
and E minor

Rhythm—Set the metronome to a desired tempo. Tap and count aloud with confidence! Feel a forward direction in your counting.

DID IT!

Rhythm Flash!—Plan the first example for 10 seconds. Then close the book and tap the rhythm. Do the same for the second example.

DID IT!

Sight reading—Notice the rhythm of the four phrases in the left hand. Set the metronome to ♩=108 and tap the rhythm. Then play without stopping!

DID IT!

Key of _____

FJH22

Rhythm—Add the bar lines, and then tap and count aloud with energy! Then, using the E natural minor scale, play the example.

DID IT! ☐

Pattern Flash!—First, block each chord group. Are you playing 1st or 2nd inversion chords? Then play as written.

DID IT! ☐

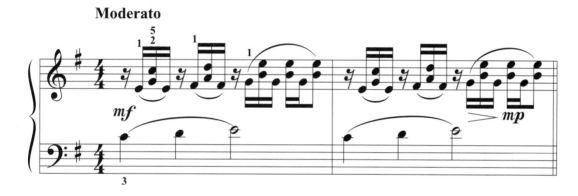

Sight reading—Plan the left-hand chords with a blocked or broken pattern. Play the melody until the fingering is easy. Then play as written with a steady tempo.

DID IT! ☐

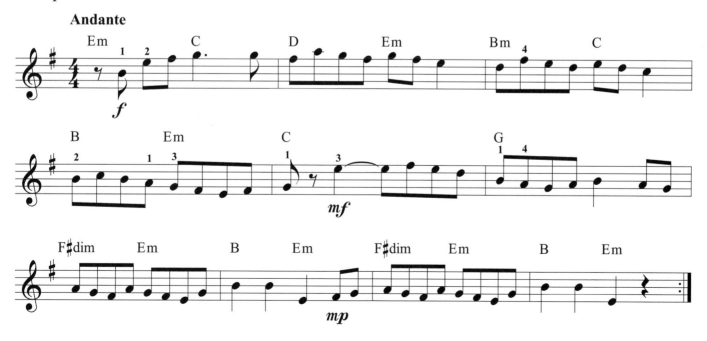

Rhythm—Tap the following rhythm slowly and evenly. When secure, tap it faster. Can you improvise using the key of E minor—chords in the left hand and melody in the right hand?

DID IT!

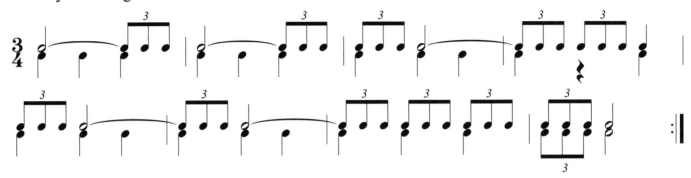

Chord Flash!—Play each chord blocked. Add fingering if needed. Then play as written with a steady tempo.

DID IT!

Sight reading—Block the left-hand chords. Then play the melody as beautifully and as legato as you can. Play the left hand more quietly than the right hand. Look at the music and not at your hands.

DID IT!

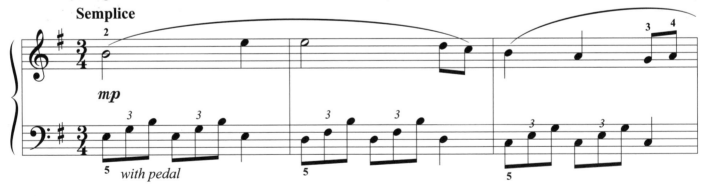

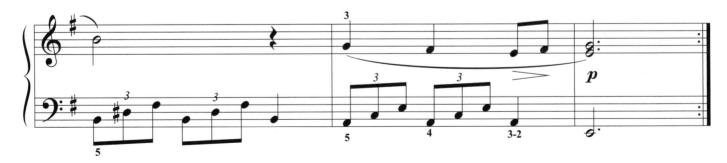

Rhythm—Tap this rhythm at two tempos of your choice.

♩ = _____   ♩ = _____

DID IT! ☐

Pattern Flash!—Prepare each example carefully. Don't forget the F♯.
Can you play each from memory?

DID IT! ☐

Sight reading—Plan your own fingering and dynamics. Write them in
if you need to. Then play as written.

DID IT! ☐

Moderato

5

 Rhythm—Stand up and march to the ♪ beat. Clap the rhythm evenly. ♪ = 100, then ♪ = 108. **DID IT!**

 Rhythm Flash!—Plan the following example for 20 seconds or less. Then close your eyes and tap the rhythm. **DID IT!**

 Sight reading—Choose a tempo that you can keep steady. Tap the rhythm hands together, counting aloud ♩ = 126. **DID IT!**

FJH2241

Ensemble Piece

DID IT!

The / / / means to play the same ostinato pattern throughout the measure. Plan the chords blocked first, then play as written.

Gray Skies

Teacher accompaniment (student plays as written)

? After playing, ask yourself, "Were my teacher and I in sync with each other?"

Unit 6

Review of ledger line reading

Review of ledger line reading

Rhythm—Sway to the ♩. beat while clapping the rhythm. ♪ = 112

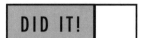

Rhythm Flash!—Study the first example for 10 seconds or less. Then close your eyes and clap it from memory. Do the same with the second example.

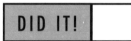

Sight reading—Notice the repeated motives in the right hand. What intervals will you play? Silently plan the left-hand moves. Then choose a tempo that you can be successful at and play as written.

DID IT!

FJH2241

Rhythm—With the metronome set at ♪ = 132, tap the following rhythm. Choose any two triads and play it while counting aloud.

DID IT!

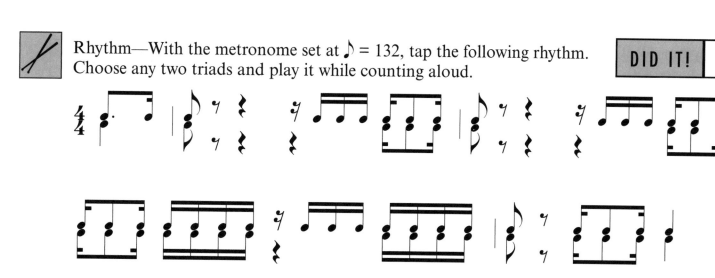

Pattern Flash!—Block the right-hand chords, naming each one aloud. Plan the fingering. Don't look down at your hands as you play.

DID IT!

Sight reading—Plan the key and the accidentals. Play without looking at your hands, and from the beginning to the end without stopping.

DID IT!

Moderato

Rhythm—With the metronome set at ♪=100 point to each note and speak the lyrics with energy!

DID IT!

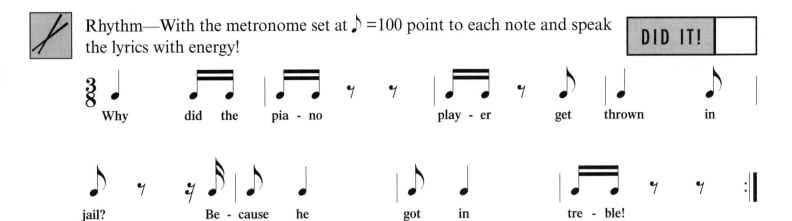

Interval Flash!—Can you name the following intervals as you play them?

DID IT!

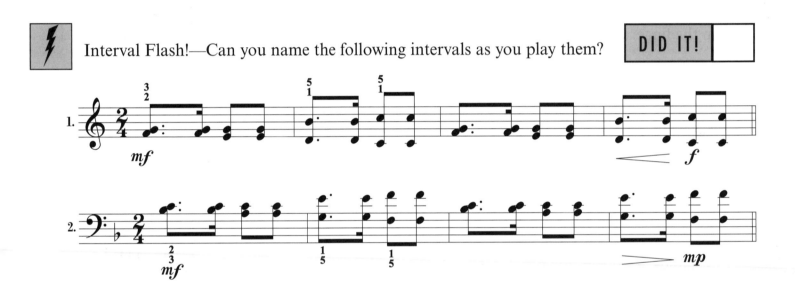

Sight reading—Plan the right-hand fingering. Play the piece silently on top of the keys while counting aloud. Look at the music and not at your hands!

DID IT!

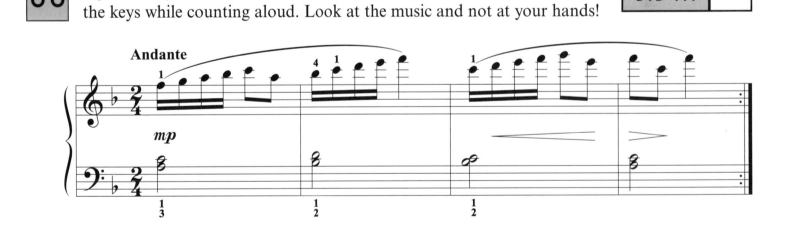

Rhythm—Tap the right hand while stomping your left foot and count the following rhythm as evenly as you can.

DID IT! ☐

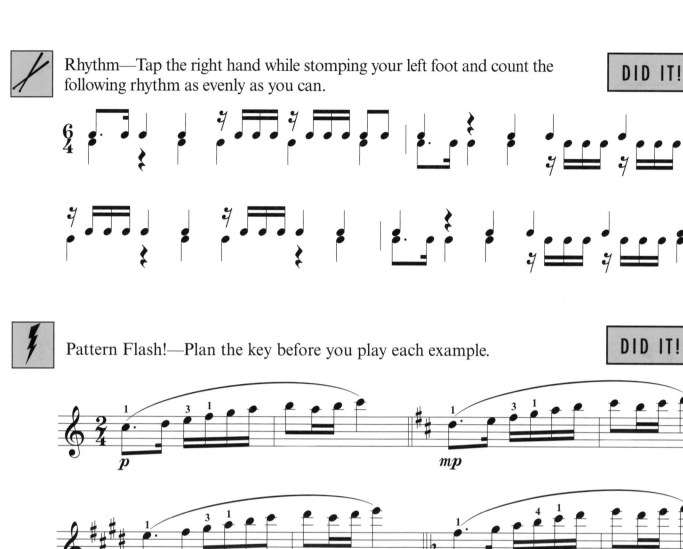

Pattern Flash!—Plan the key before you play each example.

Sight reading—Plan the key and the left-hand chords. On downbeats without chord symbols, replay the preceding chord. Then tap and count the right-hand rhythm. Once you start, don't stop until the very end.

DID IT! ☐

Andante

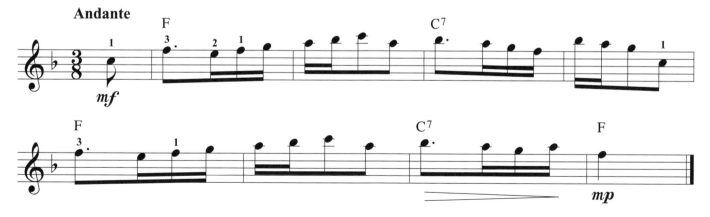

Rhythm—Add bar lines to the following rhythm. Then clap and count with energy!

DID IT!

Sight reading—Study the following example for 20 seconds. Can you name the right-hand intervals while you play?

DID IT!

Allegro

Sight reading—Plan the key. Then say the left-hand intervals while you play the left hand. Lastly, play hands together.

DID IT!

Moderato

Sight reading—Plan the key and the accidentals. Then play with confidence, always looking ahead.

DID IT!

Andante

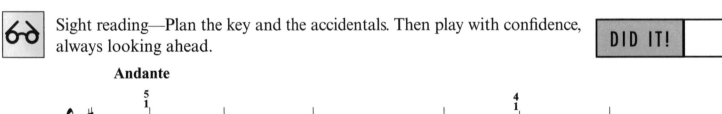

Ensemble Piece

DID IT!

Before playing, plan the time and key signatures, and the rhythms. Notice the motivic patterns which include repeated notes, descending intervals, and ♪♫♫ scale passages.

Classical Theme

Teacher accompaniment (student plays as written)

? After playing, ask yourself, "Did we play with energy and rhythmic precision?"

Unit 7

Review of relative keys of B♭ major and
G minor

Rhythm—At a ♪ =116, tap the rhythm first with your left hand; then on
the repeat, with your right hand.

DID IT!

Rhythm Flash!—Tap and count each example. Plan a tempo that you can
keep steady. After you tap each one, close your eyes and try to remember it.

DID IT!

1 (e) + a 2 e (+) a

1 e + a 2 e + a 3 e + a 4 e + a

Sight reading—Before playing, plan the key signature and rhythm. Tap hands
together keeping a steady tempo, looking at the music. Add your own
dynamics when you play the piece.

DID IT!

FJH2224

Rhythm—How quickly and accurately can you tap this rhythm hands together?   DID IT! ☐

Pattern Flash!—Play a B♭ major scale—first, right hand, then left hand. Take 20 seconds to plan the rhythm and fingering of the first example, and then play it. Do the same for the second example.   DID IT! ☐

Sight reading—Silently play the piece on top of the keys while counting. Then play as written without stopping.   DID IT! ☐

Key of _____

Largo

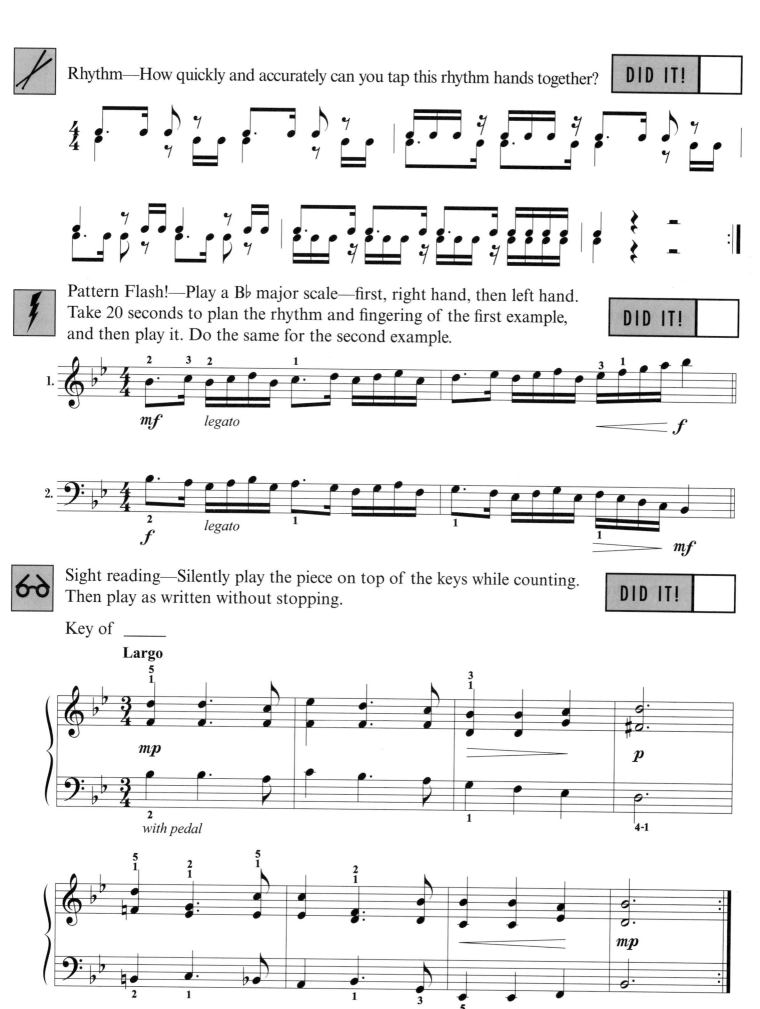

Rhythm—Tap the right hand and stomp your left foot for the left-hand notes.
♪ = 116.

DID IT!

Interval Flash!—Block each chord first. Can you write in the name
of the chords? Then play as written.

DID IT!

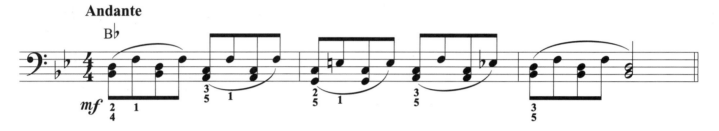

Sight reading—Keeping a steady rhythm, play the left hand as written,
blocking the right hand (except measure 4!). Then play as written.

DID IT!

Key of _____

FJH224

Rhythm—With the metronome set at ♪ = 132, tap the following rhythm. Snap your fingers whenever you see an "x". **DID IT!**

 Pattern Flash!—Notice the sequence (same pattern moving up or down by step) in both hands. Play the following example, being sure to subdivide the dotted rhythms. Can you play it again in the key of F major? **DID IT!**

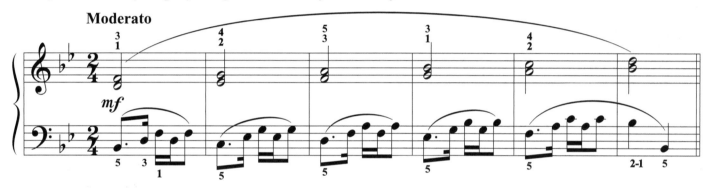

 Sight reading—Can you play this piece without any fingerings marked in? Plan it before you begin, and once you start, don't stop, always looking at the music. **DID IT!**

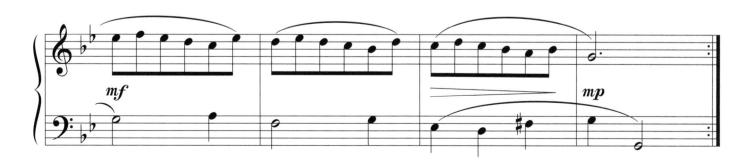

Rhythm—Tap the following rhythm. Snap where you see a ✗.   DID IT! □

 Sight reading—How are the first two measures similar? Give yourself one chance to play this example correctly, so plan well before you start.   DID IT! □

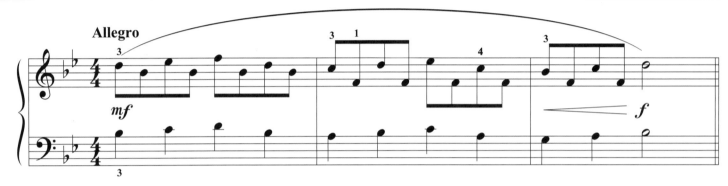

 Sight reading—Plan the right-hand chords, and then the left-hand bass line. Then play the entire piece silently on the top of the keys. Once you are confident, play it without stopping.   DID IT! □

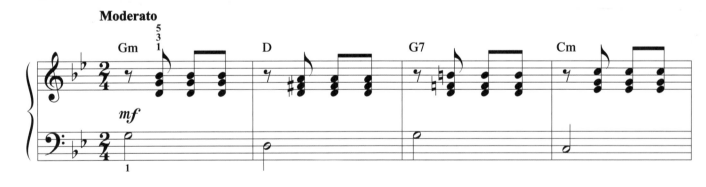

FJH2241

Ensemble Piece

DID IT!

Tap and count the rhythm at a steady tempo. Can you "sing" the melody in your head before you play the piece?

Melancholy Melody

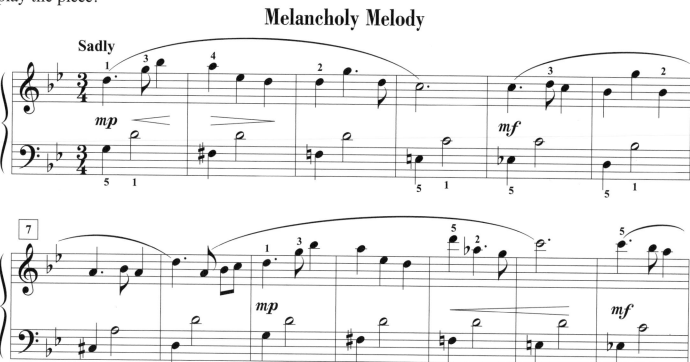

Teacher accompaniment (student plays as written)

? After playing, ask yourself, "Did I play with a steady left-hand beat?"

Unit 8

Review of relative keys of E♭ major
and C minor

Rhythm—Use the metronome at ♪ = 84 in order to help you with this rhythm.
Always count with forward direction.

DID IT!

Rhythm Flash!—Look at the first example for 10 seconds or less. Close the
book and try to remember it exactly! Do the same with the second example.

DID IT!

1.    2.

Sight reading—Count while you play and remember to subdivide the beats.
(♪ = 144) Can you "hear" the left-hand melody in your mind?

DID IT!

Moderato

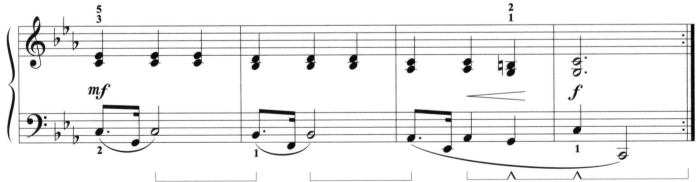

FJH2241

Rhythm—Tap and count the following rhythm with energy! Snap your fingers for each "x". ♪ = 100

DID IT! ☐

 Pattern Flash!—Look at the example and plan it for 40 seconds or less. Choose your own fingering. Then close the book and play.

DID IT! ☐

 Sight reading—Plan the left-hand chords first. Can you play this melody with a waltz accompaniment in the left hand?

DID IT! ☐

Add pedal if you like!

Rhythm—How accurately can you tap the following rhythm? ♪ = ca. 108-116. **DID IT!**

Interval Flash!—Say the intervals while you play the following example. Then close the book and play it from memory! **DID IT!**

Sight reading—Play while blocking each left-hand group. Then play as written. **DID IT!**

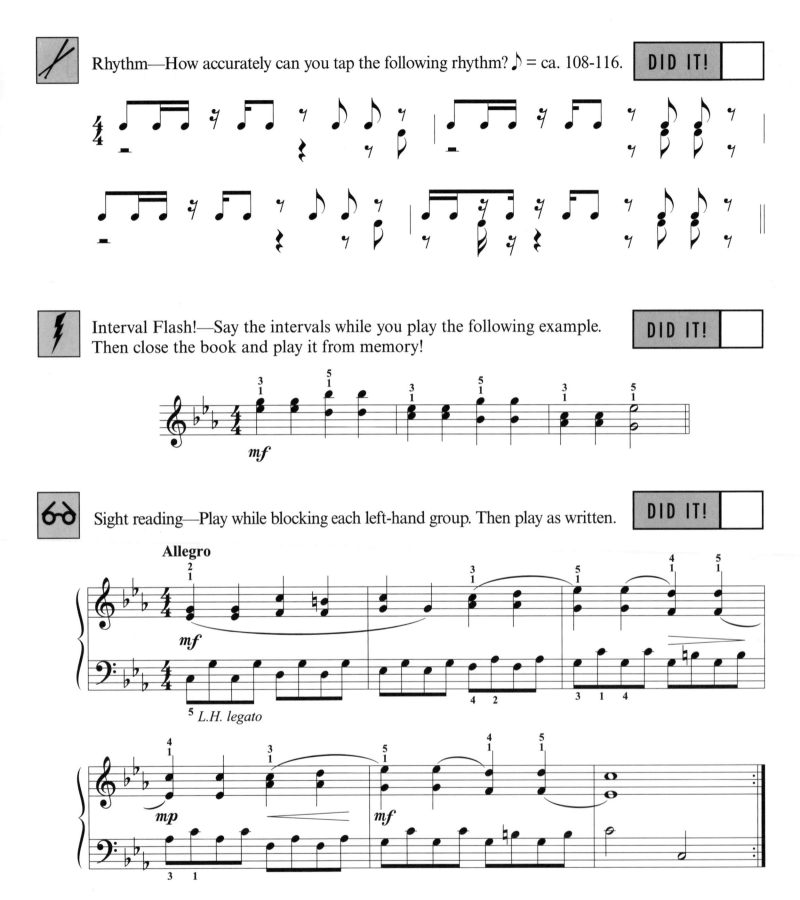

Rhythm—Say the following lyrics while pointing to each note. ♪ = 108-126   **DID IT!**

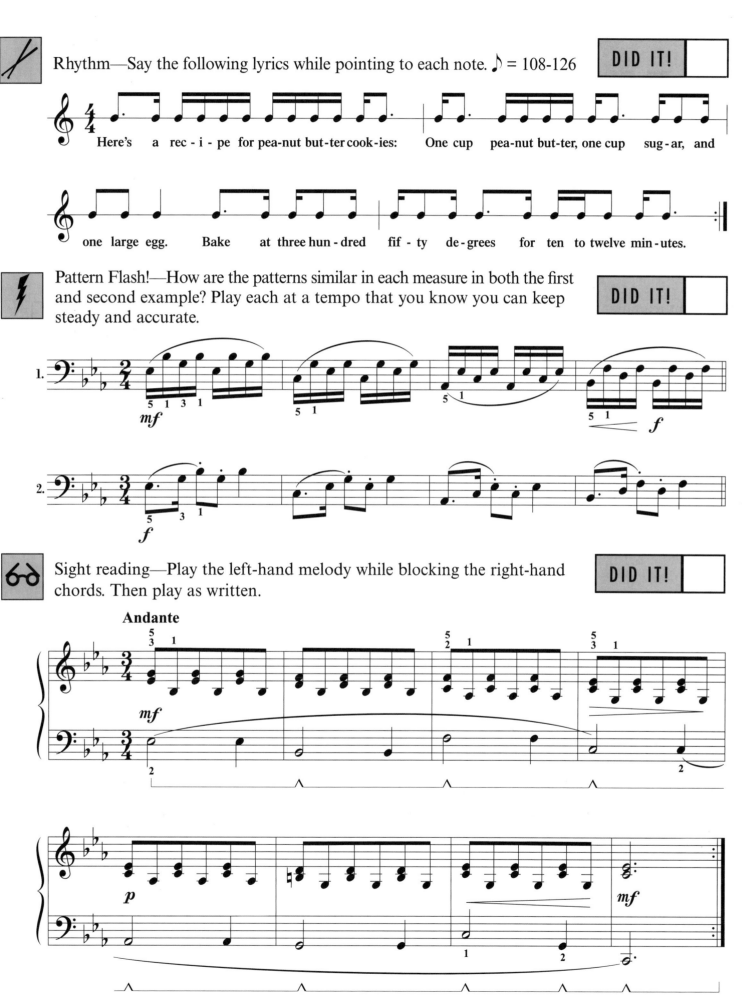

Pattern Flash!—How are the patterns similar in each measure in both the first and second example? Play each at a tempo that you know you can keep steady and accurate.   **DID IT!**

Sight reading—Play the left-hand melody while blocking the right-hand chords. Then play as written.   **DID IT!**

Andante

Rhythm—Fill in the blank measures. Then tap and count aloud!

 Sight reading—Think through the piece while counting. Choose a tempo that will allow you to be successful.

Ensemble Piece

DID IT!

Before you play as written, block all the chords in the right hand. Play the left-hand melody as beautifully as you can.

Mountain Stream

Teacher accompaniment (student plays as written)

? After playing, ask yourself, "Did I sight read this piece feeling the chord shapes underneath my fingers as I kept my eyes on the music?"

Unit 9

⭐ Review of relative keys of A♭ major and F minor

Rhythm—Clap the following with confidence! ♩ = 72   DID IT! ☐

Rhythm Flash!—Look at this rhythm for 20 seconds or less. Tap it, then close the book and try to tap it again from memory.   DID IT! ☐

Sight reading—Tap and count the rhythm before you play.   DID IT! ☐

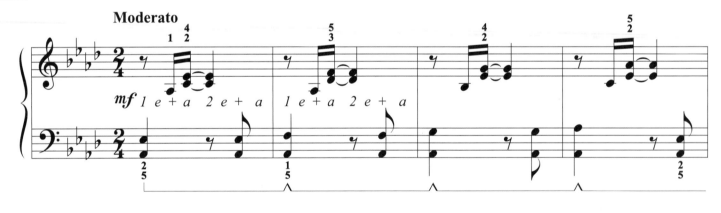

FJH2241

Rhythm—Fill in the unfinished measures. Then clap and count with energy in your voice! ♩=72

DID IT!

 Pattern Flash!—Plan the rhythm and the key signature. After playing it once, try to play it again from memory.

DID IT!

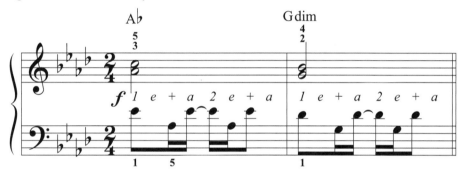

Sight reading—Once you begin this piece, don't stop until the very end. Keep your eyes on the music throughout.

DID IT!

Rhythm—Tap this rhythm evenly on the fallboard of the piano! ♩ = 96   **DID IT!**

Chord Flash!—Plan the fingering and the key signature. After you play the first example, try to play it again from memory. Do the same with the second example.   **DID IT!**

Sight reading—With the ♪ = 72, silently play this example first. Can you "hear" the melody in your head?   **DID IT!**

Rhythm—Set the metronome to a desired tempo. Tap and count with confidence! ♩ = 96-104

DID IT!

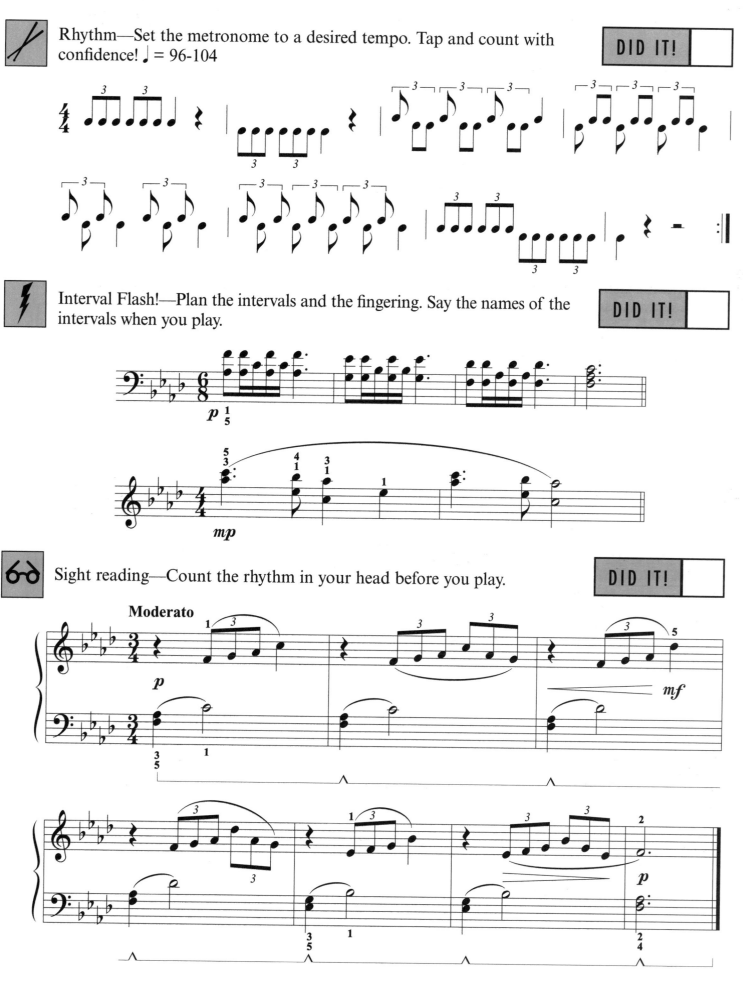

Interval Flash!—Plan the intervals and the fingering. Say the names of the intervals when you play.

DID IT!

Sight reading—Count the rhythm in your head before you play.

DID IT!

Rhythm—Add the bar lines and then tap and count with energy. ♩= 92-104   DID IT!

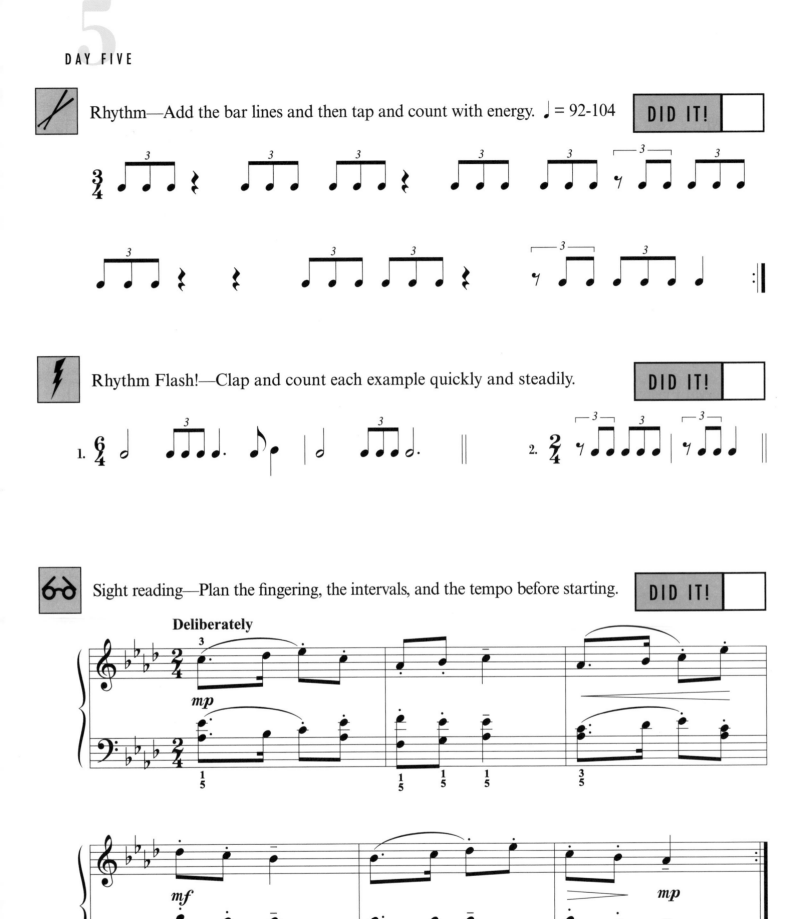

Rhythm Flash!—Clap and count each example quickly and steadily.   DID IT!

Sight reading—Plan the fingering, the intervals, and the tempo before starting.   DID IT!

Deliberately

mp

mf

mp

FJH22

Ensemble Piece

DID IT!

Before you begin, plan the key signature and the chords. Once you start, don't stop until you reach the very end! Keep it very steady.

Hoedown

Teacher accompaniment (student plays as written)

? After playing, ask yourself, "Did I keep going no matter what, and was the piece steady?"

Review of ledger line reading

Rhythm—Tap the following rhythm with the metronome at ♩ = 76. It will be easier if you count aloud.

DID IT! ☐

Interval Flash!—Look at the first example for 10 seconds or less. Then close the book and tap it from memory. Do the same with the second example.

DID IT! ☐

Sight reading—Silently plan the right-hand starting pitch and the left-hand chords. Then play without stopping!

DID IT! ☐

FJH2241

Rhythm—Set the metronome at ♩ = 69, and then tap and count aloud.

DID IT! ☐

 Pattern Flash!—How are the two pattern flashes different? Once you plan these, play them!

DID IT! ☐

 Sight reading—Plan the right-hand melody and the left-hand chords. Practice the chords with pedal.

DID IT! ☐

Adagio

Rhythm—Clap this rhythm at two tempos of your choice.

DID IT!

Interval Flash!—Plan the first example silently for 20 seconds. Then close the book and play it. Do the same for the second example.

DID IT!

Sight reading—Plan the key and time signature before starting. Once you begin, look at your music and not at your hands.

DID IT!

Leggero

mp molto legato e cantabile

Rhythm—Clap the rhythm as evenly as you can. For every "X", snap your fingers. ♪=100

DID IT!

Pattern Flash!—Prepare the patterns before you play. Look ahead at your music and not down at your hands.

DID IT!

Andante

Sight reading—Play this piece without stopping. Always keep a steady beat and don't worry about mistakes.

DID IT!

Gently

Rhythm—Complete the empty measures with your own rhythm. Then devise a left-hand melody using this rhythm in the key of B♭ major.

DID IT!

Sight reading—Before beginning, choose a tempo that you can keep steady.

DID IT!

Sight reading—Plan the chords in the right hand by blocking each group.

DID IT!

FJH224

Ensemble Piece

Before playing, plan the key and time signatures. Silently play on the top of the keys with the metronome clicking ♩ = ca. 92.

It's Time for Popcorn

Teacher accompaniment (student plays as written)

? After playing, ask yourself, "Did I keep going, no matter what little mistakes I made?"

Unit 11

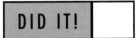

Review of relative keys of A major and
F♯ minor

 Rhythm—Clap the rhythm evenly and accurately. ♪ = ca. 100 | DID IT!

 Rhythm Flash!—Tap and count each example. Then close the book and tap them from memory! | DID IT!

 Sight reading—With the metronome set at ♪ = 112, clap the rhythm of the right-hand melody until secure. Count while you play and remember to subdivide the beats. | DID IT!

Rhythm—Clap and count the following rhythm with energy in your voice!
♪ = ca. 100-112

DID IT!

 Pattern Flash!—Learn the pattern below in the keys of A and G major.
Then continue the pattern on F and E♭.

DID IT!

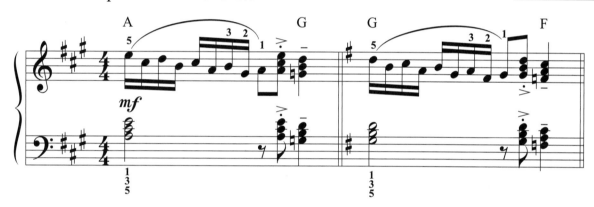

 Sight reading—Play the right hand as beautifully as possible. Block the
left-hand chords.

DID IT!

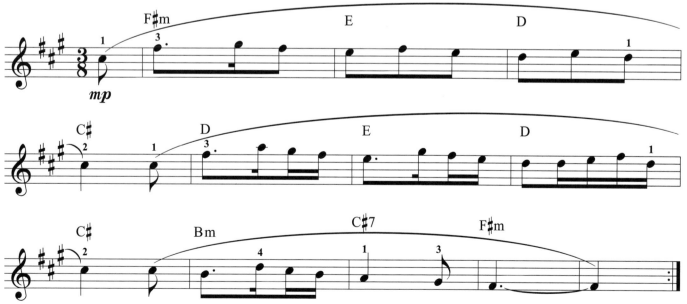

Rhythm—Fill in the empty measures. Then clap and count with energy!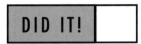

 Interval Flash!—Look at this example for 10 seconds or less. Then close the book and play it from memory.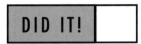

 Sight reading—Add the left-hand fingering if you need to. Silently play the piece on top of the keys, blocking the right-hand notes. Once you begin, play with confidence until the end!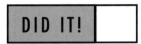

FJH2241

Rhythm—Say the following lyrics while pointing to each note. ♪ = 100

DID IT!

Rhythm Flash!—Count the rhythm of the first example in your head. When you think you can do it from memory, close the book and try it! Do the same with the second example.

DID IT!

Sight reading—Plan the key. Play without looking at your hands. Always look ahead.

DID IT!

Rhythm—Fill in the unfinished measures with notes or rests. Choose one metronome marking to tap the rhythm evenly: ♩ = 100 or ♩ = 108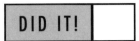

 Interval Flash—Say the intervals as you play them.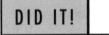

 Sight reading—Silently play this example first. Decide your own dynamics. Look at the intervals and the chord shapes as patterns.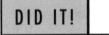

FJH224

Ensemble Piece

DID IT! ☐

Your teacher will give you 1-2 minutes to prepare this piece silently.

Piano Bench Rag

Teacher accompaniment (student plays as written)

? After playing, ask yourself, "Did I keep a steady beat?"

Unit 12
Sight Reading and Rhythm Review

Can you sing the melodies in your head? (Give yourself the first pitch and see!)

Plan both pieces before playing. When you think that you can play each successfully, play with confidence.

DID IT!

FJH224

Major Scales Flash—Plan the fingering and the key signature for each scale before you begin.

DID IT!

Sight Reading Chord Flash—Plan the left-hand chords. Can you improvise a simple melody in the right hand over the ostinato pattern?

DID IT!

Pattern Flash—Plan this example for 20 seconds. After you play it, close your eyes and try it again from memory.

DID IT!

Rhythm—Clap and count with energy in your voice!
♪ = ca. 104

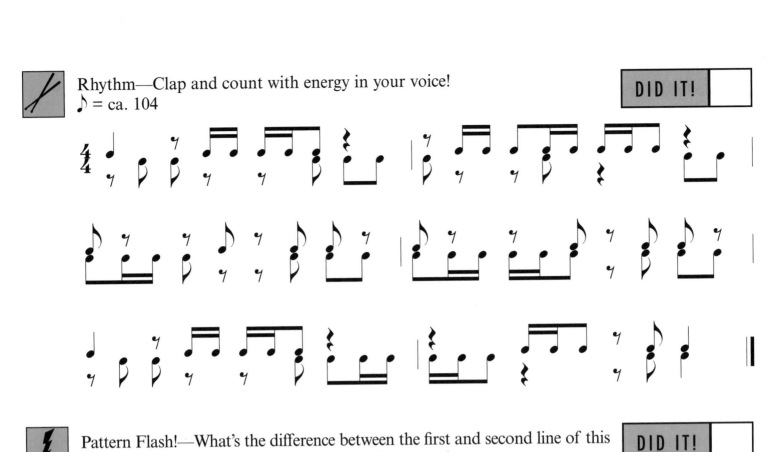

Pattern Flash!—What's the difference between the first and second line of this example? Plan the moves and then play with a steady tempo.

Sight Reading—First, silently play on the top of the keys for accuracy. Think through the rhythm in your mind.

Moderato

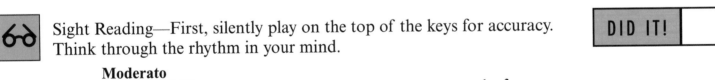

FJH22

Pattern Flash—Notice the sequences in the music. Play slowly enough (without looking at your hands) that you can be 100% accurate.

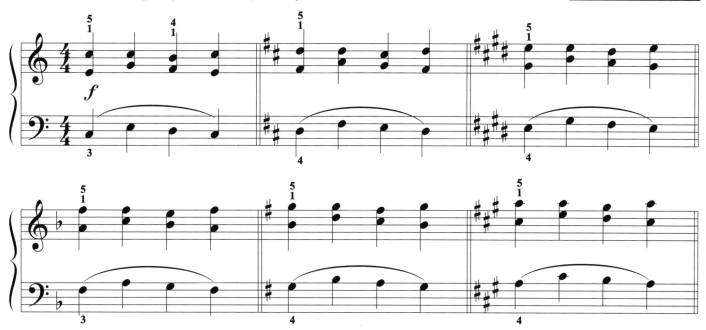

 Sight Reading—Silently plan the left-hand chords. Then use the waltz pattern and play as written. Add your own dynamics.

DID IT!

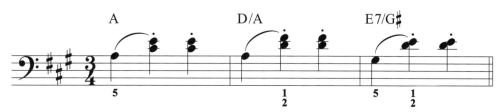

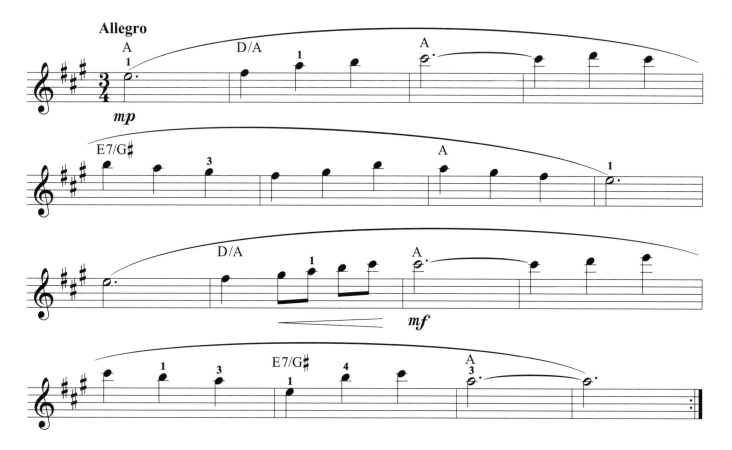

Rhythm—Tap each example quickly and accurately. ♩ = ca. 76

1.

2.

3.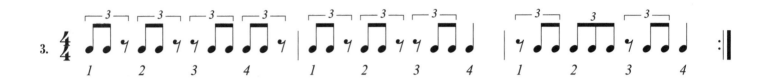

 Sight reading—Play silently on the top of the keys for accuracy. Practice the moves.

Andante

Adagio

Allegretto

Notice the repeated patterns in both hands.
Plan the intervals throughout and the chord shapes.
Play the piece silently on the top of the keys for one minute and then play aloud.

F. Beyer
from *Elementary Instruction Book*

Certificate of Achievement

_____

has successfully completed

SIGHT READING &
RHYTHM EVERY DAY®

BOOK 7

of The FJH Pianist's Curriculum®

You are now ready for **Book 8**

_____
Date

_____
Teacher's Signature